THE COLDEST PLACE
ON EARTH

At the South Pole today there is a building called the Amundsen–Scott Station. Inside the building it is warm and people live and work there both in summer and in winter. Planes fly easily to and from the station, and the rest of the world is only a few hours away. But walk five hundred metres away from the station, and Antarctica is once again the coldest, emptiest place on earth.

In 1911 there were no planes and no buildings at the South Pole. There was nothing. Only snow and ice and wind. There was no British flag, and no Norwegian flag. But across the ice, men were moving slowly south. Scott's men had ponies, and Amundsen's men had dogs and skis. The temperatures were $-30°$ Centigrade and worse. The men were tired, hungry, cold . . . Who was going to be the first man at the South Pole?

Inside the Amundsen–Scott Station today, there are some words written on the wall – words that Captain Scott wrote in his diary in 1912:

'Great God! This is an awful place.'

OXFORD BOOKWORMS LIBRARY
True Stories

The Coldest Place on Earth

Stage 1 (400 headwords)

Series Editor: Jennifer Bassett
Founder Editor: Tricia Hedge
Activities Editors: Jennifer Bassett and Alison Baxter

TIM VICARY

The Coldest Place on Earth

OXFORD UNIVERSITY PRESS

OXFORD
UNIVERSITY PRESS

Great Clarendon Street, Oxford OX2 6DP

Oxford University Press is a department of the University of Oxford.
It furthers the University's objective of excellence in research, scholarship,
and education by publishing worldwide in

Oxford New York

Auckland Cape Town Dar es Salaam Hong Kong Karachi
Kuala Lumpur Madrid Melbourne Mexico City Nairobi
New Delhi Shanghai Taipei Toronto

With offices in

Argentina Austria Brazil Chile Czech Republic France Greece
Guatemala Hungary Italy Japan Poland Portugal Singapore
South Korea Switzerland Thailand Turkey Ukraine Vietnam

OXFORD and OXFORD ENGLISH are registered trade marks of
Oxford University Press in the UK and in certain other countries

ISBN 978 0 19 478903 5

A complete recording of this Bookworms edition of
The Coldest Place on Earth is available on audio CD ISBN 978 0 19 478838 0

Typeset by Oxuniprint
Printed in China

The publishers would like to thank the following
for their permission to reproduce photographs:
Norsk Polarinstitutt: pages 15, 17, 25, 32
Popperfoto: pages 3, 7, 10, 14, 18, 23, 29, 30, 31, 35, 36, 38
The Royal Geographical Society: pages 2, 11, 12, 19, 20, 34

Word count (main text): 5500 words

For more information on the Oxford Bookworms Library,
visit www.oup.com/bookworms

CONTENTS

Chapter 1

Two Ships

The race began in the summer of 1910.

On June 1st, in London, a black ship, the *Terra Nova*, went down the river Thames to the sea. Thousands of people stood by the river to watch it. They were all excited and happy.

On the *Terra Nova*, Captain Robert Falcon Scott smiled quietly. It was a very important day for him. He was a strong man, not very tall, in the blue clothes of a captain. He was forty-one years old, but he had a young face, like a boy. His eyes were dark and quiet.

One man on the ship, Titus Oates, smiled at Scott.

'What an exciting day, Captain!' he said. 'Look at those people! I feel like an important man!'

Scott laughed. 'You *are* important, Titus,' he said. 'And you're going to be famous, too. We all are. Do you see this flag?' He looked at the big British flag at the back of the ship, and smiled at Oates. 'That flag is coming with us,' he said. 'In the Antarctic, I'm going to carry it under my clothes. We're going to be the first men at the South Pole, and that flag is going to be first, too!'

* * * * *

Five days later, on June 6th, a man opened the door of his wooden house in Norway. He was a tall man, with a long face.

Captain Robert Falcon Scott

He waited outside the house for a minute. Everything was very quiet. He could see no houses, only mountains, trees, and water. It was nearly dark. The sky was black over the mountains.

The man smiled, and walked quickly away from the house, down to the sea. In the water, a big wooden ship waited for him. The man got onto the ship, and talked and laughed quietly with his friends.

The ship's name was *Fram*, and the man was Roald Amundsen. The *Fram* was the most beautiful ship on earth,

Roald Amundsen

Amundsen thought. His friends were the best skiers on earth, too. One of them, Olav Bjaaland, smiled at him.

'North Pole, here we come, Captain,' he said.

'Yes.' Amundsen said. His friends could not see his face in the dark. '*Fram* is going to the Arctic.'

Everyone on the *Fram* was ready to go to the North Pole, to the Arctic. Amundsen wanted to go there, too. But first he wanted to go south. His friends didn't know that.

At midnight on June 6th, the *Fram* moved quietly away from Amundsen's house, out to sea.

Chapter 2

The Race

T he *Fram* went to an island in the south of Norway. It was a very little island, with only one small wooden house, two trees – and nearly a hundred dogs.

'Look at that!' Bjaaland said. 'It's an island of dogs! There are dogs in the water, near the trees, on the house – dogs everywhere!'

Two men came out of the house. 'Hassel! Lindstrøm!' Amundsen said. 'It's good to see you! How many dogs do you have for me?'

'Ninety-nine, Roald,' said Hassel. 'The best ninety-nine dogs from Greenland. And they're very happy! They don't work;

they just eat and play all day! They're having a wonderful summer here!'

'Good, good.' Amundsen laughed. 'But that's finished now. Hey, Bjaaland! Stop laughing – come down here and help me. Let's get all these dogs onto the ship!'

It was not easy. The dogs were fat and strong, and they didn't want to go on the ship. But at last, after three hours' hard work, all ninety-nine were on the ship, and the *Fram* went out to sea again.

The men were not happy. The weather was bad, the dogs were dirty, and some of the men were ill. They began to ask questions.

'Why are we bringing dogs with us?' asked one man, Johansen. 'We're going thousands of kilometres south, past Cape Horn, and then north to Alaska. Why not wait, and get dogs in Alaska?'

'Don't ask me,' said his friend, Helmer Hanssen, 'I don't understand it.'

The men talked for a long time. Then, on September 9th, Amundsen called everyone to the back of the ship. He stood quietly and looked at them. Behind him was a big map. It was not a map of the Arctic. It was a map of Antarctica.

Bjaaland looked at Helmer Hanssen, and laughed. Then Amundsen began to speak.

'Boys,' he said. 'I know you are unhappy. You often ask me difficult questions, and I don't answer. Well, I'm going to answer all those questions now, today.

'We began to work for this journey two years ago. Then, we wanted to be the first men at the North Pole. But last year, Peary, an American, found the North Pole. So America was first to the North Pole, not Norway. We're going there, but we're too late.'

'I don't understand this,' Bjaaland thought. 'Why is Amundsen talking about the North Pole, with a map of Antarctica behind him?'

Amundsen stopped for a minute, and looked at all the men slowly. No one said anything.

'We have to go a long way south before we get to Alaska,' he said. 'Very near Antarctica, you know. And Captain Scott, the Englishman, is going to the South Pole this year. He wants to put his British flag there. An American flag at the North Pole, a British flag at the South Pole.'

Bjaaland began to understand. He started to smile and couldn't stop. He was warm and excited.

'Well, boys,' Amundsen said slowly. 'Do we want the British to put their flag at the South Pole first? How fast can we travel? We have a lot of dogs, and some of the most wonderful skiers on earth – Bjaaland here is the best in Norway! So I have an idea, boys. Let's go to the South Pole, and put the Norwegian flag there before the British! What do you say?'

For a minute or two it was very quiet. Amundsen waited, and the men watched him and thought. Then Bjaaland laughed.

'Yes!' he said. 'Why not? It's a ski race, isn't it, and the English can't ski! It's a wonderful idea, of course! Let's go!'

Chapter 3

The Ponies

On October 27th, the *Terra Nova* arrived in Wellington, New Zealand. When Scott came off the ship, a newspaper man walked up to him.

'Captain Scott! Captain Scott! Can I talk to you, please!' he said.

Terra Nova

Scott stopped and smiled. 'Yes, of course,' he said. 'What do you want to know?'

'Are you going to win?' the man asked.

'Win?' Scott asked. 'Win what?'

'Win the race to the South Pole, of course,' the newspaper man said. 'It's a race between you and Amundsen, now. Look at this!' He gave a newspaper to Scott. Scott looked at it. It said:

FRAM RACES SCOTT TO SOUTH POLE

'We're going to win!' says Amundsen

Scott's face went white. 'Give me that!' he said. He took the newspaper and read it carefully. The newspaper man watched him, and waited. 'Well, Captain Scott,' he said at last. 'Who's going to win this race? Tell me that!'

Scott looked at him angrily. 'This is stupid!' he said. 'It's not a race! I came here to learn about the Antarctic – I'm not interested in Amundsen, or in races!' Then he walked back onto his ship, with the newspaper in his hand.

Later that day, he talked to his men. He gave them the newspaper, and laughed.

'It doesn't matter,' he said. 'We're in front of Amundsen, and we have more men, and more money. He has only eight men, and a lot of dogs. I know about dogs – they don't work in the Antarctic. We have sixteen men and the new motor sledges – they are much better. And tomorrow the ponies are coming. We need ponies, motor sledges, and good strong British men – that's all. Forget about Amundsen! He's not important!'

Scott asked Oates to look after the ponies, but he did not let Oates buy them. When Oates first saw the ponies, in New Zealand, he was very unhappy. Most of the ponies were old, and some of them were ill.

'They're beautiful ponies, Titus,' Scott said. 'They come from China – they're wonderful ponies!'

Oates looked at them angrily, and said nothing. Then he asked: 'Where is their food, Captain?'

'Here!' Scott opened a door.

Oates looked inside. He thought for a minute. 'We need more food than this, Captain Scott! These ponies are going to work in the coldest place on earth – they need a lot of food – more than this!'

Scott smiled quietly. 'We can't take more food on this ship, Titus. Where can we put it? But it doesn't matter, old boy. They're very strong ponies, you know. The best ponies on earth.'

Later that night, Oates wrote a letter to his mother. *There are nineteen ponies on the* Terra Nova *now*, he wrote. *All the ponies are in a small room at the front of the ship. We eat our food in the room under the ponies, so our table is often wet and dirty. Scott makes a lot of mistakes, I think, and Antarctica is a very dangerous place.*

Oates and the ponies on the Terra Nova

Chapter 4

Food Depots

The two ships, *Terra Nova* and *Fram*, arrived in Antarctica, in January 1911, at the end of summer. The Englishmen and the Norwegians wanted to stay on the ice all winter. They wanted to be ready to go to the South Pole at the beginning of the next Antarctic summer.

The dogs pulled the Norwegians' sledges. They ran quickly over the snow and pulled the big sledges from the ship onto the ice. The men ran beside them on skis.

They put a big wooden house on the ice. The house was full of food, and skis, and sledges. They called it Framheim.

Framheim

Outside the house, the dogs lived in holes under the snow. When the house was ready, the men made their first journey south.

Before the winter, they wanted to take a lot of food south, and leave it in depots. For the long journey to the Pole, they needed a lot of food, and they couldn't carry it all with them. On February 10th, five men, three sledges, eighteen dogs, and half a tonne of food left Framheim and went south.

It was easy. The weather was warm for the Antarctic, between −7° Centigrade and −17° Centigrade. The snow was good, and the dogs and skis went fast. They went fifty or sixty kilometres every day. After four days they reached 80° South, and made the first depot.

Amundsen made his depot very carefully. It was very important to find it again, next summer. So he put a big black

The first depot

flag on top. Then he put ten flags to the east of the depot – each flag half a kilometre from the next – and ten flags to the west. So there were flags for five kilometres to the left of the depot, and five kilometres to the right.

Then they went back to Framheim, and took some more food south, this time to 82° South.

This time it was harder. The temperature was sometimes –40° Centigrade, and there were strong winds with a lot of snow. The dogs and men were very tired, and the tents and boots were bad. At the second depot, they put out sixty flags, to help them find it again.

They came back to Framheim on March 23rd. It was nearly winter in the Antarctic. Their ship *Fram* was far away now, near South America. They were alone on the ice.

* * * * *

Oates went with Scott to make the first British depot. They left Cape Evans on January 25th. There were thirteen men, eight ponies, and twenty-six dogs. The dogs were faster than the ponies – they ran quickly over the top of the snow, but the ponies' feet went through it. Every morning the ponies started first, and the dogs started two hours later, because they ran faster. At night, the dogs made warm holes under the snow, but the ponies stood on top of the snow. It was –20° Centigrade.

After fifteen days Oates talked to Scott. There was a strong wind, and the two men's faces were white with snow.

'Three of these ponies are ill, Captain,' Oates said. 'They can't go on.'

'Don't be stupid, Oates,' Scott answered. 'They're good strong animals – the best ponies on earth.'

'Not these three,' Oates said. 'They're ill, and unhappy, and now they can't walk. Let's kill them, and leave the meat here, in the snow. We can eat it, or the dogs can.'

'Of course not!' Scott said angrily. 'These ponies are our friends, they work hard for us. I don't kill my friends!'

Three days later, two of the ponies were dead.

Scott's men were slower than Amundsen's; it took them twenty-four days to get to 80° South. They made a big depot there, and put one large black flag on top of it. Then they went back to Cape Evans.

Terra Nova *at Cape Evans*

Their camp was on an island in the ice, and the sea ice moved sometimes. There were holes in the ice, and black sea water under it. One day seven ponies went through the ice into the sea, and died. One motor sledge also went into the sea.

Chapter 5

A Long Cold Winter

It was dark for four months. Outside the wooden house at Framheim, it was often −60° Centigrade. The dogs lived in warm holes under the snow. The men stayed in the house, and worked in their rooms under the snow.

The skis and sledges came from the best shops in Norway, but Bjaaland wasn't happy with them. He changed a lot of things on the skis and sledges. Soon the sledges were stronger than before. The skis were better and faster, too.

All the Norwegians

Bjaaland changed a lot of things on the sledges.

worked hard. They looked after their dogs, and worked on their equipment – the sledges, skis, tents. Every day they thought about their journey to the Pole, and talked about it. And every day, Amundsen thought about Scott. One day, in midwinter, he talked to his men.

'Let's start early, before Scott,' Amundsen said. 'Remember, Scott has more men than us, and he has motor sledges, too. Perhaps they can go faster than us.'

Bjaaland laughed. 'Oh no, they can't go faster than me,' he said. 'On snow, nothing can go faster than a good man on skis.'

'We don't know,' Amundsen said. 'You're the best skier in Norway, but you get tired, and dogs get tired, too. Motor sledges don't get tired. They can go all day and all night.'

Johansen laughed angrily. 'That's stupid,' he said. 'Perhaps the motor sledges can go all night, but the Englishmen can't. The English can't win, Roald – they don't understand snow, but we do. And they're too slow.'

'Perhaps,' Amundsen said. 'But I want to win this race. So we're going to start early! Do you understand?'

It was quiet and warm inside Framheim. Bjaaland looked at Amundsen, and thought about the long, cold journey in front of him. He thought about the dogs in their holes under the snow, and listened to the wind over the house. 'When, Roald?' he said quietly.

'On August 24th. The sun comes back on that day. We start then.'

'But we can't!' Johansen said. He looked angry, and

Inside Framheim

unhappy. 'That's too early! We can't start then – it's dangerous and stupid!'

Amundsen looked at Johansen coldly. 'You're wrong, Johansen,' he said. 'We want to win, remember? So we start on August 24th.'

Bjaaland listened to the winter wind outside.

* * * * *

In Scott's camp, at Cape Evans, no one talked about Amundsen and no one worked hard. They had good food, and they played football on the snow. They wrote a newspaper – *The South Polar*

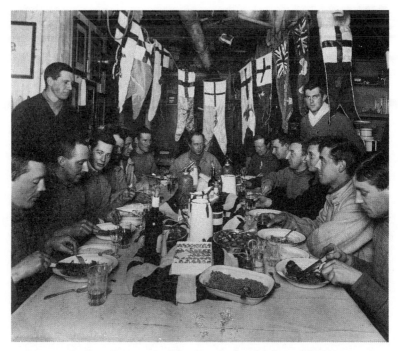

In Scott's camp at Cape Evans they had good food.

Times – and read books. No one learnt to ski, no one worked on the motor sledges. Twice, men went for long journeys across the snow. They walked, and pulled the sledges themselves. Oates stayed at Cape Evans and looked after his ponies.

Over the window in Cape Evans, Scott put a map of Antarctica. With a pen, he made a line from Cape Evans to the South Pole, and he put a little British Flag at the Pole. Under the map, Scott wrote the day for the start of their journey.

We start on November 3rd, he wrote.

We start on November 3rd, *he wrote*.

Chapter 6

A Bad Start

On August 23rd, the Norwegians' sledges were ready. They took them outside, and the dogs pulled them across the ice. The sun came up for a half an hour, but it was too cold: −46° Centigrade. They could not travel in that weather. They went back to Framheim and waited.

They waited two weeks, until September 8th. Then, with the temperature at −37° Centigrade, they started. They ran happily across the snow to the south – eight men, seven sledges, and eighty-six dogs. Only Lindstrøm, the cook, stayed behind in Framheim.

At first everything went well. They went twenty-eight kilometres on Saturday, and twenty-eight kilometres on Sunday. It was easy.

At first everything went well.

Then, on Monday, the temperature went down – to –56° Centigrade. There was white fog in front of their faces. They couldn't see anything. But they travelled twenty-eight kilometres.

That night, in their tents, they nearly died of cold. Next day, they stopped and made snow houses. Inside the snow houses, it was warm. But everyone was unhappy.

'I told you, Roald!' Johansen said. 'Even September is too early! We can't travel in this cold. Do you want us to die? Let's go back and wait for better weather.'

Amundsen was very angry. He was angry with Johansen, but he was angry with himself, too. He knew Johansen was right.

'All right,' he said slowly. 'We can go on to the depot at 80° South, leave the food there, and then go back. We can't do more than that.'

It was thirty-seven kilometres to the depot. The wind was in their faces all day. Two dogs died on the way. At the depot, they did not stop. They put out the food and the flags, turned round, and went north.

At last the wind was behind them. The dogs ran quickly, and the men sat on the empty sledges. They went faster and faster. It was like a race. Amundsen was on Wisting's sledge, and soon he, Wisting, and Hanssen were three or four kilometres in front. Soon they were alone. They travelled seventy-five kilometres in nine hours, and they reached Framheim at four o'clock that afternoon.

Bjaaland arrived two hours later, with two more men. But the last two – Johansen and Prestrud – went more slowly. Their dogs were tired, their feet were wet and cold, they had no food, and they were alone in the dark. The temperature was −51° Centigrade. They reached Framheim at midnight.

Next morning, Johansen was angry. In front of everyone, he said: 'You were wrong, Roald. September was too early. I told you but you didn't listen. And then you left us alone and we nearly died in the cold! You're a bad captain – I'm a better captain than you are!'

Amundsen was very angry. But at first he said nothing, because he knew that Johansen was right. Then, that evening, he gave a letter to Johansen. It said:

You aren't coming to the Pole with me. When I go south, you can take some dogs and go east to King Edward VII Land. You can go with Prestrud and Stubberud. You can be the first men to go there – but not to the South Pole!

The Norwegians stayed in Framheim and waited. They lay in bed, listened to the wind outside, and thought about Scott and his motor sledges.

Chapter 7

Motor Sledges and Mountains

Scott had two motor sledges now. They were the first motor sledges in the Antarctic – the first on earth. On October 24th, the motor sledges started south from Cape Evans. Four men went with them, but Scott stayed at Cape Evans for another week.

Oates was unhappy. He wrote to his mother: *We had a very bad winter here. I don't like Scott. We were here all winter, but he didn't learn to ski, or to drive dogs. Our equipment is bad, and he doesn't think about other people. I'm going to sleep in his tent on the journey, but I don't want to.*

The first motor sledge in Antarctica

On November 1st Scott and Oates and six more men left Cape Evans with eight sledges and eight ponies. The ponies walked slowly because their feet went down into the snow. It was hard work for them and they got tired very quickly. They travelled thirteen or fourteen kilometres in a day.

Behind the ponies came Meares with one sledge and some dogs. Meares knew how to drive dogs. Every day, Meares started two hours after the ponies, and arrived two hours before them.

After five days, they found the motor sledges.

* * * * *

The Norwegians began again on October 20th. There were five men this time – Amundsen, Bjaaland, Wisting, Hassel, and Hanssen. They had four sledges, and forty-eight dogs.

There was a lot of wind and fog. On the first day, Wisting's sledge suddenly stopped, and the back went down. 'Come on, you dogs!' he said angrily. 'Pull! Pull!' At first nothing happened; then, slowly, the sledge moved again. Wisting looked down, over the side of the sledge. Under the snow, there was a fifty metre hole.

'Did you see that?' Amundsen said. 'The ice wants to eat us – men, dogs, sledges, everything.'

On the fourth day they reached the depot at 80° South. There was a bad snowstorm, but they found the flags easily. Next day the men stayed in their tents, and the dogs played in their holes under the snow. They were all happy. They had a lot of food, they had good equipment, and they were warm. They could travel fast.

The depot at 80° South.

Next morning, the snowstorm stopped, and the journey began again. *Today, everything is wonderful*, Bjaaland wrote in his diary. *But where is Scott? In front of us, or behind?*

* * * * *

There was no one with the motor sledges; they were broken. Scott looked at them angrily.

'It doesn't matter,' he said. 'Teddy Evans and his men are in front of us. They're good men – they're pulling their sledges themselves. We can get to the Pole on foot.'

Oates looked at Meares. Oates and the ponies were tired, but Meares and his dogs were not. The snow was home for them.

That night, Oates wrote: *Three motor sledges at £1,000 each, 19 ponies at £5 each, 32 dogs at £1.50 each. Well, it's not my money, it's Scott's.*

On November 21st, one of the ponies died.

* * * * *

On November 11th, the Norwegians saw the mountains.

The mountains were very high – some of the highest on earth. Bjaaland smiled.

'There is good skiing up there, Roald,' he said. 'But can dogs get up there too?'

'Of course they can,' Amundsen said. 'Come on.'

They left Hanssen with the dogs, and skied a little way up the mountains. It was difficult, but the mountains were big and beautiful. Behind the mountains, Amundsen thought there was a high plateau of ice. 'That's it,' Amundsen said. 'That's the road to the Pole. Tomorrow, we can bring the dogs and sledges up here. But now, let's have a ski race. Who can get back to camp first?'

They laughed, and skied happily down the white snow. 'This is like home,' Bjaaland thought. 'But it's bigger than Norway, and better.'

In the next four days, the dogs pulled the sledges eighty-one kilometres, and went up 3,000 metres. At last, Amundsen and Bjaaland stood on the plateau behind the mountains. They were tired, happy men.

Bjaaland looked back at the mountains. 'Can a motor sledge get up here?' he asked.

Amundsen smiled. 'No,' he said. 'I don't think so. And Scott doesn't like dogs. So his men are going to pull their sledges up these mountains themselves. Would you like to do that, Olav?'

Bjaaland didn't answer. He smiled, and skied happily away across the snow.

Chapter 8

Across the Plateau

On November 21st, the Norwegians killed thirty dogs. 'They were happy,' Amundsen said. 'And now they're going to die quickly. We need three sledges, and eighteen dogs, to go to the Pole.'

When the dogs were dead, the other dogs ate them. The men ate them, too. *They were good friends*, Bjaaland wrote in his diary. *And now they are good food.* Two days later, the dogs were fat. Then, in a snowstorm, they began the journey again.

After the snowstorm, there was fog, and in the fog, they got lost on an ice river with hundreds of big holes in it. They could see nothing, and it was very dangerous. In four days they moved nine kilometres. *But the ice is beautiful*, Bjaaland wrote. *Blue and green and white. This is a wonderful place – but I don't want to stay a long time.*

After the ice, there were strong winds and bad snowstorms. They could see nothing in front of them. But every day, they travelled twenty-five or thirty kilometres. Then, on December 9th, the sun came out. They were at 88° 23' South – 175 kilometres from the Pole.

Five more long days, Bjaaland wrote. *That's all now. But where is Scott?*

* * * * *

For four days, Scott's men stayed in their tents near the mountains. *There is a bad snowstorm outside*, Oates wrote. *It's too cold for the ponies, and our clothes and skis are bad, too.*

On December 9th, Oates killed the ponies. They were tired and ill and they could not walk up to the plateau. Then Meares and his dogs went back to Cape Evans. 'We can pull the sledges ourselves,' Scott said. 'We can do it – we're all strong men.'

There were two sledges and eight men. They went twenty-four kilometres a day. On December 31st, Scott said to Teddy Evans, and the men on the second sledge: 'You can't ski well.

'We can pull the sledges ourselves,' Scott said.

Leave your skis here.' So they pulled their sledge twenty-four kilometres without skis.

Next day, Scott went to Teddy Evans's tent. 'You are ill, Teddy,' he said. 'You can't come to the Pole. Take two men and go back, tomorrow.'

Teddy Evans was very unhappy. 'Two men, Captain?' he said. 'Why not three?'

'Because Bowers is going to come with me,' Scott said. 'He's strong – we need him.'

'But . . . you have food on your sledge for four men, not five!' Evans said. 'And Bowers has no skis!'

'I'm the Captain, Teddy!' Scott said. 'You do what I say. Take two men and leave Bowers with me!'

Oates wrote to his mother: *I am going to the Pole with Scott. I am pleased and I feel strong.* But in his diary he wrote: *My feet are very bad. They are always wet now, and they don't look good.*

On January 4th Scott's men left Teddy Evans and went on. Scott, Oates, Wilson and Edgar Evans had skis, but Bowers did not. They were 270 kilometres from the Pole.

They were 270 kilometres from the Pole.

* * * * *

December 14th 1911 was a warm, sunny day. Five Norwegians skied over the beautiful white snow. It was very quiet. No one spoke. They were excited, and happy.

'Six more kilometres,' Bjaaland thought. *Is there a British flag? I can't see a flag, but . . .*

'Look!' Hassel said. 'What's that over there?'

Bjaaland left his sledge and skied quickly away over the snow. 'What is it?' he thought. 'Is it . . .? No!'

'It's nothing!' he called. 'There's nothing there . . . nothing!'

Three kilometres, two. 'Roald!' Hanssen called to Amundsen. 'Go in front of me, please. It helps my dogs.'

'That's not true,' Bjaaland thought. 'His dogs are running well today. But Hanssen wants Amundsen to be first. The first man at the South Pole!'

They skied on and on, over the beautiful snow.

'Stop!' Amundsen said. He waited quietly for his men. 'This is it,' he said.

Bjaaland looked at him. 'But there's nothing here,' he said.

Amundsen smiled. 'Oh

'This is it,' said Amundsen.

yes there is,' he said. 'There's something very important here, Olav. Very, very important.'

'What's that, Roald?'

'Us. We're here now. Isn't that important, Olav?'

The four men stood on the snow, and looked at him. Then, slowly, they all began to laugh.

Chapter 9

The End of the Race

The Norwegians stayed two days at the Pole. They left a tent there, with a Norwegian flag on it. Inside the tent, they left some food, a letter for the King of Norway, and a letter for Scott.

The Norwegians left a tent with a flag on it.

They left some more black flags near the Pole, and one twenty-eight kilometres north. Then they skied away, back to the north.

It's a beautiful day, Bjaaland wrote. *The sun is warm, the snow is good. But the dogs run too quickly – I can't get in front of them!*

They found their depots easily. There were ten between the Pole and Framheim. Each depot had a lot of food. They laughed and skied quickly down the mountains. Often, they skied fifty kilometres a day. On Friday, January 26th, 1912, they came back to Framheim. It was four o'clock in the morning.

Inside the wooden house, Lindstrøm, the cook, was asleep. Amundsen walked quietly to his bed. 'Good morning, Lindstrøm,' he said. 'Is our coffee ready?'

* * * * *

The black flags waited at the Pole.

'What's that, Captain?' Bowers said. 'Over there?'

'Where?' Scott asked. 'What – oh my God!'

They all saw the small black flag in the snow, two kilometres in front of them. Slowly, they pulled their sledge to it.

Next day, January 17th 1912, they found the tent and the Norwegian flag. Near it, Scott took the British flag from under his clothes, and put it up. In his diary, Scott wrote: *This is a very bad day. We are all tired, and have cold feet and hands. It is –30°*

On January 17th 1912, they found the tent and the Norwegian flag.

Centigrade and there is a snowstorm. Great God! This is an awful place!

They turned north. Five tired, unhappy men, in the coldest, emptiest place on earth.

Five tired, unhappy men, in the coldest, emptiest place on earth.

* * * * *

On March 13th, 1912, Scott's wife Kathleen, looked at her morning newspaper. NORWAY'S FLAG AT SOUTH POLE, it said. She looked at it for a long time, and then began to cry.

'What's the matter?' her friend asked.

'My poor, poor husband,' Mrs Scott said. 'What's happened to him? Where is he now?'

* * * * *

Scott's men were always hungry. There were not many depots and they were difficult to find. *We need to find the next depot today*, Oates wrote. *But how can we find one black flag in all this snow? It's very difficult. And there is food for four men, not five.*

Scott's men were always hungry.

They were all tired and ill, too. Oates's feet were black now, and he could not feel them. On February 16th, Edgar Evans died.

On the 17th they were past the mountains. At the depot there they ate one of the dead ponies. Then they went on – ten, eleven, twelve kilometres a day. They were ill because their clothes were not warm and they didn't have much food. The temperature was sometimes –40° Centigrade.

On March 7th Scott looked at Oates's feet. They were big and black. 'I can't pull the sledge now,' Oates said. 'It's very difficult to walk. Am I going to lose these feet, Captain?'

Scott looked at Oates's feet, and said nothing.

On March 9th they found another depot, but there was not much food. Slowly, they walked on. Oates's feet were worse every day.

March 17th was Oates's birthday. He was thirty-two. He lay in the tent and listened to the wind outside. He was very cold, very hungry, and very very tired.

He wrote a letter to his mother and gave it to Wilson. Then he got up, and opened the door of the tent. He stopped in the door for a minute. Scott, Wilson, and Bowers looked at him. They didn't speak.

'I'm going outside for a minute,' Oates said. 'I may be some time.'

They didn't see him again.

* * * * *

At Cape Evans, the Englishmen waited. On December 11th, Meares and the dogs came back. On January 3rd, Teddy Evans and his two men arrived at Cape Evans. The *Terra Nova* came, and went. Winter began. Scott did not come.

The Englishmen waited all winter at Cape Evans. Then, on October 26th 1912, they started for the south. Two weeks later, they found a tent.

There were three bodies in the tent – Scott,

They put the bodies under the snow.

Wilson, and Bowers. They put the bodies under the snow. Then they took the men's letters and diaries, and went north to Cape Evans again.

In Scott's diary they read: *Oates died like a good Englishman. We all did. Please, remember us, and look after our families. We did our best.*

No one found Oates's body. But he is there, somewhere, under the snow and the wind, in the coldest, emptiest place on earth.

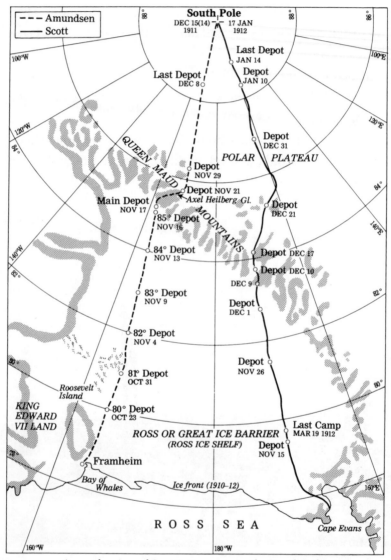

Amundsen's and Scott's journeys to the South Pole.

GLOSSARY

alone if you are alone, you are the only person there
awful very, very bad
boot a big strong shoe
broken when an engine cannot move, it is broken
buy to give money for something
camp a place to stay
captain the most important man on a ship
dangerous something dangerous can kill or hurt you
depot a place to leave food and equipment
diary a book; you write in this what you did every day
Earth the world; our planet
empty with nothing in it
equipment the things you need (e.g. skis, boots, sledges)
flag a piece of cloth with a special pattern on it; every country
    has its flag
fog thick, cloudy air near the ground
go on to continue (not stop)
God (my God) words you say when you are unhappy or afraid
great very important, or very good
hard difficult
hole where you can see through something
ice water that is hard because it is very cold
island a piece of land with sea all round it
journey going from one place to another place
king the most important man in a country
last (at last) in the end
lie (past tense lay) to go down on the ground
line a row of people or things (e.g. the depot flags were in a
    line)
look after (with animals) to give them food and take care of
    them

lost   when you are lost, you do not know where you are

map   a drawing of the land, which shows where things are

mistake   when you do the wrong thing

motor sledge   a sledge with an engine, like a car

mountain   a very big hill

plateau   a high, flat place on a hill

Pole (the South Pole)   the exact bottom of the Earth

pony   a small horse

poor   when you say 'poor', you are feeling sorry for somebody

pull   to make something move

race   when two or more people try to be first

reach   to arrive; to get somewhere

ski *(n)*   a long piece of wood under your shoes, for travelling across snow

skier   a person who travels on skis

sledge   something to carry food and equipment across the snow

snow   soft white stuff that falls from the sky when the weather is very cold

snowstorm   a lot of wind and a lot of snow

start   to begin; to take the first step

stupid   not clever

temperature   how hot or cold it is

tent   a small house made of cloth

travel   to go from one place to another place

unhappy   not happy

win   to be first in a race

wind   air that moves

wooden   made of wood, from trees

The Coldest Place on Earth

ACTIVITIES

ACTIVITIES

Before Reading

1 **Read the story introduction on the first page of the book, and the back cover. How much do you know now about the story? Tick one box for each sentence.**

	YES	NO
1 A race to the North Pole began in 1910.	☐	☐
2 Scott was English and Amundsen was Norwegian.	☐	☐
3 There was nothing at the South Pole in 1911.	☐	☐
4 All the travellers returned home after their journey.	☐	☐
5 Scott wrote: 'The South Pole is a beautiful place.'	☐	☐
6 Scott and Amundsen stayed in the Amundsen–Scott Station.	☐	☐
7 Today, you can fly to the South Pole.	☐	☐

2 **What is going to happen in the story? Can you guess? Tick one box for each sentence.**

	YES	NO	PERHAPS
1 Nobody gets to the South Pole.	☐	☐	☐
2 Scott gets to the South Pole first.	☐	☐	☐
3 Amundsen gets to the South Pole first.	☐	☐	☐

	YES	NO	PERHAPS
4 Amundsen dies in the Antarctic.	☐	☐	☐
5 Scott dies in the Antarctic.	☐	☐	☐
6 Scott finds Amundsen and helps him.	☐	☐	☐
7 Scott's men eat their ponies.	☐	☐	☐
8 Amundsen's men eat their dogs.	☐	☐	☐

3 **Can you do this crossword? All the words are in the story introduction, or under pictures in the book.**

ACROSS

1 The race was to this place. (5,4)

3 Soft white stuff that falls from the sky when the weather is very cold. (4)

4 Air that moves. (4)

6 Long pieces of wood under your shoes. (4)

DOWN

1 Something to carry things across snow. (6)

2 Small horses. (6)

5 Water that is hard because it is very cold. (3)

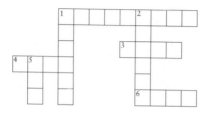

ACTIVITIES

While Reading

Read Chapters 1, 2 and 3. Who are these sentences about, Scott or Amundsen? Write in the names.

1 _____ left London on June 1st, 1910.
2 _____ left Norway on June 6th, 1910.
3 _____ wanted to have a race to the South Pole.
4 _____ wasn't interested in races.
5 _____ had eight men.
6 _____ had a lot of dogs from Greenland.
7 _____ bought ponies in New Zealand.
8 _____ had sixteen men.

Read Chapters 4 and 5, then make eight true sentences from this table.

The Norwegians The British The ponies The dogs	walked	in holes under the snow.
	worked	to ski.
	lived	on their equipment.
	didn't work	two depots with many flags.
	made	slowly through the snow.
	ran	one depot with one flag.
	didn't learn	fast over the snow.

Read Chapters 6 and 7. Then complete this passage.

The Norwegians started in _____, but they nearly died of
_____, so they went back to Framheim. They left again on
_____ 20th, with five _____, four _____, and forty-eight
_____. They travelled _____, and everybody was _____.

The British started on _____ 24th. They had two _____,
eight sledges with eight _____, and one sledge with _____.
The ponies travelled _____, and got _____ quickly. The
_____ broke, and the men _____ the sledges themselves.

Read Chapter 8, and then answer these questions.

1 What did the Norwegians kill and eat?
2 How far were they from the Pole on December 9th?
3 What happened on December 14th, 1911?
4 Which Englishmen went back to Cape Evans?
5 Who went on with Scott to the Pole?
6 How many sledges and how much food did they have?
7 How far was Scott from the Pole on January 4th?

**Before you read Chapter 9, can you guess the answers to
these questions?**

1 Do the Norwegians stay at the Pole and wait for Scott?
2 Do the Englishmen reach the South Pole?
3 Do all the Englishmen get back to Cape Evans?

ACTIVITIES

After Reading

1 **Match these halves of sentences to tell the story of the end of the race.**

1 The Norwegians got to the Pole on December 14th, . . .
2 On the way back they travelled fast, often fifty kilometres a day, . . .
3 The Englishmen reached the Pole on January 17th, . . .
4 They left the Pole and started north again, . . .
5 In March they were still a long way from home . . .
6 At Cape Evans the Englishmen waited all winter, . . .
7 In October, when the next Antarctic summer began, . . .
8 After two weeks they found a tent, with the bodies of Scott, Wilson and Bowers, . . .
9 about five weeks after the Norwegians got there.
10 but Scott and his men did not come.
11 so they were back at Framheim by January 26th.
12 the men at Cape Evans started for the south.
13 and they didn't have much food.
14 and stayed there for two days.
15 but nobody ever found the bodies of Titus Oates and Edgar Evans.
16 but they travelled slowly, about ten kilometres a day.

2 Here is a conversation between Amundsen and a reporter. Write it out in the correct order, and put in the speakers' names. The reporter speaks first (number 7).

1 _____ 'Difficult? No, but you must have a lot of flags. How many flags did Scott have at his depots?'

2 _____ 'No. There was a depot a few kilometres away, but they didn't find it. Is it difficult to find depots, sir?'

3 _____ 'All right. What do you want to ask?'

4 _____ 'Dead? No, I didn't know. What happened?'

5 _____ 'Poor men. Were they far from a depot?

6 _____ 'Sixty! So it was easy to find!'

7 _____ 'Mr Amundsen! Can I ask you some questions, please?'

8 _____ 'One? That's no good. You need lots of flags.'

9 _____ 'His friends found him in his tent, with Wilson and Bowers. They died of cold and hunger.'

10 _____ 'Well, at our second depot we had sixty flags.'

11 _____ 'One, sir. A big flag on top of the depot.'

12 _____ 'Well, first, do you know that Captain Scott is dead?'

13 _____ 'Yes, sir. Thank you very much, sir.'

14 _____ 'Very easy. We were careful, you see.'

15 _____ 'How many flags did you have at your depots, sir?'

3 **Here are two pages from Amundsen's and Scott's diaries. Use these words to fill in the gaps.**

Antarctica, depots, equipment, flag, great, happy, mountains, reach, tent, took, warm, well

AMUNDSEN'S DIARY: DECEMBER 14TH, 1911

Today was _____ and sunny, and the dogs ran _____. We are the first men to _____ the South Pole, and we are all very _____ and excited. When we stopped, we put up a _____ and the Norwegian _____. Then Bjaaland _____ some photos. _____ is a beautiful place; it is like the high _____ of Norway. We have a lot of food, our _____ is good, and there are ten _____ between here and Framheim. This is a _____ day for us, and for Norway!

awful, bad, feet, found, journey, letter, Norwegian, skis, snowstorm, temperature, travel, unhappy, weeks

SCOTT'S DIARY: JANUARY 17TH, 1912

This was a _____ day for us. The Norwegians got here first – five _____ before us. We _____ their tent, with its _____ flag, and a _____ for me from Amundsen. We are tired and _____, cold and hungry. The _____ is −30°, and there is a _____. Great God! This is an _____ place! Tomorrow we must begin the _____ back. Bowers has no _____, Evans is ill, and Oates has bad _____. We can only _____ slowly, and it is a long, long way home.

4 *'I'm going outside. I may be some time.'* These last words by
Titus Oates are very famous. But what did he *really* mean?
Look at these three meanings, and choose the best one.

   1 'I'm going outside, but I'm coming back in an hour or
     two. Please wait for me.'
   2 'Go back to Cape Evans. You can go faster without me.
     I can't walk now, and I don't want you to die, too.'
   3 'I'm dying, and I want to die out in the snow, not here
     in this tent.'

5 Who are these sentences about – the Norwegians (N) or the
British (B)?

   1 They were all good at skiing.
   2 They walked, and pulled the sledges themselves.
   3 They didn't use dogs, and their motor sledges broke.
   4 They put a lot of flags by their depots.
   5 They were always hungry and tired.
   6 They skied, and their dogs pulled the sledges.
   7 They put one flag at their depots.
   8 They tried to use ponies in the Antarctic.

6 Scott and his men lost the race and died, but Amundsen and
his men won, and lived. Why? Complete the sentences.

   The Norwegians won because _____
   The British lost because _____

ABOUT THE AUTHOR

Tim Vicary is an experienced teacher and writer, and has written several stories for the Oxford Bookworms Library. Many of these are in the Thriller & Adventure series, such as *White Death* (at Stage 1), or in the True Stories series, like *The Coldest Place on Earth*, which is illustrated by photographs taken on the actual expeditions to the South Pole. Another of his titles in the True Stories series is *Mutiny on the Bounty* (also at Stage 1), which is about Captain Bligh and his voyage to the south seas.

Tim Vicary has two children, and keeps dogs, cats, and horses. He lives and works in York, in the north of England, and has also published two long novels, *The Blood upon the Rose* and *Cat and Mouse*.

OXFORD BOOKWORMS LIBRARY

Classics • Crime & Mystery • Factfiles • Fantasy & Horror
Human Interest • Playscripts • Thriller & Adventure
True Stories • World Stories

The OXFORD BOOKWORMS LIBRARY provides enjoyable reading in English, with a wide range of classic and modern fiction, non-fiction, and plays. It includes original and adapted texts in seven carefully graded language stages, which take learners from beginner to advanced level. An overview is given on the next pages.

All Stage 1 titles are available as audio recordings, as well as over eighty other titles from Starter to Stage 6. All Starters and many titles at Stages 1 to 4 are specially recommended for younger learners. Every Bookworm is illustrated, and Starters and Factfiles have full-colour illustrations.

The OXFORD BOOKWORMS LIBRARY also offers extensive support. Each book contains an introduction to the story, notes about the author, a glossary, and activities. Additional resources include tests and worksheets, and answers for these and for the activities in the books. There is advice on running a class library, using audio recordings, and the many ways of using Oxford Bookworms in reading programmes. Resource materials are available on the website <www.oup.com/bookworms>.

The *Oxford Bookworms Collection* is a series for advanced learners. It consists of volumes of short stories by well-known authors, both classic and modern. Texts are not abridged or adapted in any way, but carefully selected to be accessible to the advanced student.

You can find details and a full list of titles in the *Oxford Bookworms Library Catalogue* and *Oxford English Language Teaching Catalogues*, and on the website <www.oup.com/bookworms>.

THE OXFORD BOOKWORMS LIBRARY
GRADING AND SAMPLE EXTRACTS

STARTER • 250 HEADWORDS

present simple – present continuous – imperative –
can/*cannot, must* – *going to* (future) – simple gerunds …

Her phone is ringing – but where is it?

Sally gets out of bed and looks in her bag. No phone. She looks under the bed. No phone. Then she looks behind the door. There is her phone. Sally picks up her phone and answers it. *Sally's Phone*

STAGE 1 • 400 HEADWORDS

… past simple – coordination with *and*, *but*, *or* –
subordination with *before*, *after*, *when*, *because*, *so* …

I knew him in Persia. He was a famous builder and I worked with him there. For a time I was his friend, but not for long. When he came to Paris, I came after him – I wanted to watch him. He was a very clever, very dangerous man. *The Phantom of the Opera*

STAGE 2 • 700 HEADWORDS

… present perfect – *will* (future) – *(don't) have to, must not, could* –
comparison of adjectives – simple *if* clauses – past continuous –
tag questions – *ask*/*tell* + infinitive …

While I was writing these words in my diary, I decided what to do. I must try to escape. I shall try to get down the wall outside. The window is high above the ground, but I have to try. I shall take some of the gold with me – if I escape, perhaps it will be helpful later. *Dracula*

STAGE 3 • 1000 HEADWORDS

... should, may – present perfect continuous – *used to* – past perfect –
causative – relative clauses – indirect statements ...

Of course, it was most important that no one should see
Colin, Mary, or Dickon entering the secret garden. So Colin
gave orders to the gardeners that they must all keep away
from that part of the garden in future. ***The Secret Garden***

STAGE 4 • 1400 HEADWORDS

... past perfect continuous – passive (simple forms) –
would conditional clauses – indirect questions –
relatives with *where/when* – gerunds after prepositions/phrases ...

I was glad. Now Hyde could not show his face to the world
again. If he did, every honest man in London would be proud
to report him to the police. ***Dr Jekyll and Mr Hyde***

STAGE 5 • 1800 HEADWORDS

... future continuous – future perfect –
passive (modals, continuous forms) –
would have conditional clauses – modals + perfect infinitive ...

If he had spoken Estella's name, I would have hit him. I was so
angry with him, and so depressed about my future, that I could
not eat the breakfast. Instead I went straight to the old house.
Great Expectations

STAGE 6 • 2500 HEADWORDS

... passive (infinitives, gerunds) – advanced modal meanings –
clauses of concession, condition

When I stepped up to the piano, I was confident. It was as if I
knew that the prodigy side of me really did exist. And when I
started to play, I was so caught up in how lovely I looked that
I didn't worry how I would sound. ***The Joy Luck Club***

BOOKWORMS · TRUE STORIES · STAGE 1

Mutiny on the Bounty

TIM VICARY

It is night in the south seas near Tahiti, and the ship HMS Bounty has begun the long voyage home to England. But the sailors on the ship are angry men, and they have swords and guns. They pull the captain out of bed and take him up on deck. He tries to run, but a sailor holds a knife to his neck. 'Do that again, Captain Bligh, and you're a dead man!' he says.

The mutiny on the *Bounty* happened in April, 1789. This is the true story of Captain Bligh and Fletcher Christian, and the ship that never came home to England.

BOOKWORMS · TRUE STORIES · STAGE 1

Ned Kelly: A True Story

CHRISTINE LINDOP

When he was a boy, he was poor and hungry. When he was a young man, he was still poor and still hungry. He learnt how to steal horses, he learnt how to fight, he learnt how to live – outside the law. Australia in the 1870s was a hard, wild place. Rich people had land, poor people didn't. So the rich got richer, and the poor stayed poor.

Some say Ned Kelly was a bad man. Some say he was a good man but the law was bad. This is the true story of Australia's most famous outlaw.